A Carnival Of Shadows

Poems and Ponderings.

Anuradha Ranjan

BookLeaf
Publishing

India | USA | UK

Made with ❤ on the BookLeaf Publishing Platform
www.bookleafpub.in
www.bookleafpub.com

Dedication

This book is dedicated to all my teachers, to all the people who have helped me, taught me and gave me a vision, a cause and a voice. And by corollary, I am grateful for my resulting adventure of discovery through the two languages that I learnt, French and Italian, which have definitely played a big role in shaping me into who I am today.

Even though this was a hurried effort, and my first, the poems were a long time coming. I am happy I did this, I mean, that I published. Even if it is a small hill, it's not one I have climbed before, and that's the fun of it! It just makes me glad to express myself and know that maybe there are people even if only a few... to listen. May this be the first of many, or of at least a few such adventures!

-- ANR

Preface

"Je célébrai mon jour de fête
Dans une oasis d'Afrique
Vêtu d'une peau de girafe.
On montrera mon cénotaphe
Aux côtes brûlantes de Mozambique."

T.S. Eliot,
"Mélange Adultère de Tout"

(I will celebrate my feast day
In an African oasis
Dressed in giraffe skin.
They will show my cenotaph
On the burning coasts of Mozambique.

T.S Eliot,
An Adulterous Mix of Everything)

Acknowledgements

Thank you Rohit and Annika, the loves of my life. What would I do, and where would I be without you? Thank you for your unconditional love and encouragement, for always standing by me and cheering me on!

1. The Crossing

Hurry, scurry!
Bees to a trap.
Grits to the pole,
The running wheel,
A silent whirl--
Until it stopped.
The hum, the buzz,
Thick like a gum,
Brought to a halt
With a dull thud:
Not quite a thud,
Almost a bump.
Deaf and thick,
Not smooth and slick.

The record's scratchy end
Was nothing
Like the song.

Dry, gummy, bitter
Sulky, wobbly, wavy
Dark, woolly, foggy
Like the wads of cotton
In my head and toes.
Legs up, antennae off--
Lift off, Soul-magnet!
No more searching,
No direction,
No gravity
In this new dimension.
Only Lightness and Light,
Floating in a sea of
Cottonwool clouds!

No looking back!
There's no turning back,
As I disappear
Into a wall of air.

2. Travel Diary

" *Così tra questa*
immensità s'annega il pensier mio:
e 'l naufragar m' è dolce in questo mare."

Giacomo Leopardi, "L'infinito"

I have searched for my origins,
Travelled routes of land and sea--
Where to flies the gull,
Does he ever say?

Peaks of snow,
Deserts frozen in time
Caravanserai--
Mughal Arch of a wayside inn.
The falcon of collective memory
Circles spaces
From another era,

Swept away with time.
Almost wiped out.
And you, you are not
From these parts!
This foreign entity
Will grow on you.
Your baby eyes, wide open,
Take in the scenery.
You are now in the vortex--
The eye of the cyclone,
Circling and spiralling.
Sheherazade will not sleep tonight!
Nor for another thousand nights!

I listen carefully
To barely discern
In the unfamiliar haze,
My coordinates in time and space.

Golden sands, diamond shores,
Tropical forests in distant isles,
Where will my mind-bird come to roost
In this jungle of multifarious memories?
And the last refrain... what will it be?
A faded album, forgotten pictures,
A cup of tea on a shady balcony?
My life stretched out

On a sunny beach.
How many flights will it take
Before I alight on that fertile plain,
That dream delta?

Mother! Fruit! Eyes!
Home! Darkness! Light!
The trip of your life!
Immersed in the ocean of the mind.

3. Carnival of Shadows

Come out you all, and we will play!
Sing our song, dance, and sway,
Live and relive the moonlit magic
Of this moment.
I have dimmed the lights on purpose
In the atrium of my brain.
Tracing tunes, like catching little birds,
And retrieving words from under mossy stones.

And then, quiet music and a toast
To you my friends,
That I seem to know so well
From my childhood years--
Regaling me
Each time you come
Visiting with your wordy gifts,
Recreating for me,
My life and all your lives,

Filling my cup with the mirth
Of all experience,
In one eternal moment.

Words, colourful, like plumes,
Rioting quietly, making waves,
Poems in so many hues,
Heady or subdued.
They are poets
From from times gone by,
Who populate my friendly haunt,
Parading in the penumbra
In a Carnival of Shadows.

4. The Blighted Tree

I stand today
Blighted by hate
Burnt by chance
A victim of history
And circumstance.
But yesterday I swayed
In the garden breeze,
There was
Birdsong in the trees,
Creatures nestled in my leaves,
Singing happy and free.

But Hate came one night,
Shrouded in her cloak of lies,
Masked in her deceit.
She took me by surprise,
Struck her lightning dagger
Deep within my soul.
In that very moment,
My sap turned to coal--

My life juice dried.

My branches now hollow holes,
An empty ruin now,
I am a lonely begging fool--
My hands, up in the air,
Gnarly fingers twisted skywards in gloom
Beg for Love and Forgiveness,
They beg for Peace and Togetherness,
The birdsong still in my soul.
The green of the trees
Was the green of my leaves.
My garden bloomed in many hues--
The sap of kindness
Was the blood that ran in my veins.

5. Desert road to Eternity

"Consume my heart away; sick with desire
And fastened to a dying animal
It knows not what it is; and gather me
Into the artifice of eternity."
W. B. Yeats, "Sailing to Byzantium"

What is this journey,
If not the road I have taken--
The only one I know?
Desert road, take me
To where flowers bloom
And the sun shines
Even when it rains.

This road is long
And winding.

Sometimes I pass by
People standing,
Waving to me.
Desert folks
From unknown parts,
Smiling strangely.
My horse gallops on,
Flying, swift and silent,
Past everything.

It all seems strangely still--
The barren hills
Are dunes of sand,
Lying in wait for something--
A desert storm?
A burst of rain?
Was I here before?
And will I return again?

Looking back,
I glimpse nothing
But the path,
Snaking
Between the dunes,
Disappearing
Into a point in the sand.
In my hand I clutch

My faith-compass--
Will it steer me
Through these parts?

Eyes fixed ahead,
Without blinking
I navigate the falling night,
And race to the edge of my dream.

6. Peek - a- Boo!

« *On me dit que nos vies ne valent pas grand-chose*
Elles passent en un instant comme fanent les roses
On me dit que le temps qui glisse est un salaud
Que de nos chagrins, il s'en fait des manteaux »

Carla Bruni, «Quelqu'un m'a dit »

Count the tiger's stripes!
One, Two, Peek-a-boo!
The leopard's spots--
Three, Four, where did they go?
Time, like a blink,
Disappeared behind a bush,
Drowned like a bubble,
With a blip,
Like the sun

Slipped behind a cloud,
Smothered by the fog.

Time to dance to Time--
The dance of life!
Five, Six, fiddlesticks!
A boy whistles along
A winding path,
Whistling as he sings
His song in the wind.
The path goes on,
The song is long,
Singing here,
Winding there,
Whistling in the wind.

Round and around,
Pirouette to the sound,
Circles and spirals,
The wheel of life--
Spinning and still--
That's the point of it!

Seven, Eight, Nine!
My friend, it is Time
To wind that clock!
To tip that glass of sand,

That pours onto my hand.

He's a friend that comes and goes.
His coat though,
Hangs always at the door.

7. Fatehpur Sikri

"Jesus, Son of Mary (on whom be peace) said: The World is a Bridge, pass over it, but build no houses upon it. He who hopes for a day, may hope for eternity; but the World endures but an hour. Spend it in prayer, for the rest is unseen." – (Inscription on the Buland Darwaza, Fatehpur Sikri, Agra).

Fatehpur-- City of Triumph!
Little turrets and marble domes
Race against a cloudless sky.

Red sandstone citadel
Wearing curtains of marble lace,
Horses and camels
In the outhouse well,
Drink with regal elephants,
Crossing paths

In the dry scrub underbrush.
Eunuchs guard the harem baths,
Behind the tall mysterious walls,
And princesses from exotic lands
From Siberia to the Amazon.
Twenty thousand parchment scrolls
Sit rolled in niches lined with gold.
In the twilight hour, a call to prayer
Reverberates though the jungle air.
And lesser mortals scurry in huts,
In gratitude and humility
To pray and toil and sleep and hide.
(They know nothing of this other life.)
Their days are spent in prayer and strife.

While in the palace, robed pilgrims kneel
In a cobbled courtyard under the stars.
The brightest crescent moon is out
Like a pearly jewel from behind the clouds--
As Sufi singers strike that chord,
The palace gardens spring to life!
The throaty voice of the courtesan
Pierces the nocturnal calm,
And upward notes of music soar
Like colourful kites in the balmy night.
In airy terraces the nobles crowd,
While carpets mask the shuffle of feet,

Silken canopies shiver in the breeze.
Royal artists gather round--
Glinting costumes and the sound
Of drums and music to enthrall
Their young and handsome emperor.

Named like Allah, he is great,
A conqueror and philosopher.
And like Allah the Almighty
He too is kind to this city.
But unlike Allah All- knowing,
His mortal soul is unaware,
Eyes shut in trance, senses perfumed--
That the day is close, when Fatehpur
Will be a ghost of stone and air.
Its giant doors ajar,
Like the gaping mouth
Of a waterless well.

Only the cackle of parakeets,
Crowded on the empty roofs,
Will remain to tell the story--
Singing garbled songs of lost glory.

8. Papa...

"Phlébas, le Phénicien, pendant quinze jours noyé,
Oubliait les cris des mouettes e la houle de Cornouaille,
Et les profits et les pertes, et la cargaison d'étain:
Un courant de sous-mer l'emporta très loin,
Le repassant aux étapes de sa vie antérieure.
Figurez-vous donc, c'était un sort pénible;
Cependant, ce fut jadis un bel homme, de haute taille"

T.S. Eliot, "Dans le Restaurant

Yes, I surrender now.
My battle-worn body,
My pricking thumbs,
And all my scars.
My failing eyes
And all my woes.
As I ascend ,
Leaving them,

I transcend time
In an inverted hurricane,
Passing pieces
Of spacelessness.
This is the moment
When you kill
The drone engine
And lie still.
My mind now
But a cup emptied
Of its contents--
Scattered like my ashes
In the delta
Of my Life-River.
Like the Phoenician sailor,
I revisit my life.
I must admit, though,
It's been a good flight.

9. Cardan's Rings

Like the puzzle
Of the Cardan Rings,
Generations come
And they go.
Waxing and waning,
Swelling and receding,
Like familiar tides.
History repeats
Nostalgic tunes,
People, places, events,
Familial, familiar refrains
Rehashed into different versions
Of themselves.
Sometimes with minor improvements,
At times kamikaze accidents,
Almost always, though,
Agonizingly, the same.

The antiquated record-player
Plays a tune I can't forget.

I lose myself in alleyways,
Blind with no exit,
Looking for an opening,
Circling and spiralling,
Like a vulture heaving
In the vectors of a cyclone
Dwindling and crowding
The skyline of my brain,
Covered in a blanket of rain.

And then at times, the mind's eye
Can see it clear as day!
The chain of generations--
A continuum of closed ends--
Even a couple of scattered links,
And the point of it all--
The fictive centre of all these circles--
The Light of all Experience--
Free from this unending chain--
The Escape,
The Eye, The OCULUS!

10. Funeral

Who are these people?
Why are they gathered?
Precipitating,
Like ants,
Circumambulating,
Coming to terms
With coming to term.
Like bits to a needle,
Drawn to an empty eye.
Cluttered,
Like a magnetic dust,
They stare at Nothingness,
With no understanding.
Shuddering,
As they contemplate a vacuum
That makes no sense.

Another one down,
But still no answers here.

Yet here you are--
To get a piece of me.
Amphitheatre of grim spectators,
Whispering, waiting,
For the spectacle
Of my departure.

Maestro on the centre-stage!
Dim the lights, please.
From their density,
I draw lightness.
From their confusion,
Clarity.
The waves of my life-flood
Have ebbed away.
It's been a long wait
On the shores of memory.
The slate is washed clean now.
A new sun and another dawn.
We can all go home.

11. Ode to Kerela

I would like to spend my days
In this lovely coconut haze--
Among green leaves and branches
Breathing the forest air.
Cloud kissed, perfumed
Bouquets of tea,
And endless lagoons
That lazily meet the sea,
Calling me,
Meandering endlessly,
Under sun kissed palms
And the balmy breeze, taking me
Where I want to be.

Dreaming lazily in a boat,
Watching the world float by,
My sleepy eye,

Waiting to catch a fish,
Like a wish
Caught in a moment,
Slinks and slides
Across silky waters.
The music of crickets
In the thicket,
The scent of jasmine
In the night,
And this starry firmament,
Will be my guide
And show me my way!

12. The Train

When I was little,
I got a train.
It was red and whistled,
And ran on tracks
That looped and went around,
Only to come right back!
Round and round,
It puffed and chugged,
And it always returned
To the start.

By now I've taken many trains,
Trains from here
And trains to there,
Trains to stations everywhere.
Stations come and stations go
But life's tracks are not circles,
They are lines,
That cross and wind

With other lines
They find along the way.

We pass by hills and forests green,
We whizz past things we barely see.
At times the train goes very slow--
Almost still, painfully so.
And we wish it would go fast again,
See villages go by in the rain.

The train of Life is a marvelous thing,
With a beginning and an end!
'Tis a train that gives us wings,
Unfolding lovely things
As we go by.
Some near some far,
And sometimes we may
Cross someone who will
Accompany us on the journey.

Seated in the train of Life,
Waiting for the destination,
I cannot but
Appreciate the ride,
And all the myriad moments
Until the final station.

13. GAZA

"The horror! The horror!"
(Colonel Kurtz in 'Heart of Darkness' by Joseph Conrad)

Our eyes of glass
Are stony shards,
Cold witnesses to this madness--
Dry and open,
Like an old wound--
Silently watching
Dusty rubble.

No cries,
No beating, no pounding.
Our hearts beat though,
Over the screams
And the putrid air,

Smoke, ash, and anger.
The dusty staring face
Of hunger--
Empty trees,
Skeletal canopies--
Once thoughts lived here
Like bees.

No more years of fear,
No more girls
Behind the door,
Weeping snivelling.
We hide no more,
We wait at the gate
For the enemy--
To prevail,
And leave us sunless,
Shivering,
Picking for crumbs.

The clock stopped--
No one to wind it now.
The key, lost--
No one to find it now.
We, the forgotten.
How will we forget
The horror,

The carnage,
The hunger,
The razing of us
To the ground?

And now we watch
Your eyes too
Turn to shards--
Glassy stones
With no memory,
And no emotion.

14. The Long Wait

Four winters have I seen
My friend,
Winters with no end
To that wretched feeling
Of sorrow
And injustice,
And hushed whispers in dark places.
I have waited
Through these lonely nights,
I have prayed
For freedom.
Winters without end
Inhabit these cells.

I shout my pain.
And while I pray,
I hear the cackle
Of those who gleefully prey
On innocents.

Many were lost
In these four winters--
Mostly to treachery.
Even while brazen voices
Heated the winter nights,
Giving hope to the hopeless,
Piercing the fog of deceit and lies,
I just lay silently waiting
In a frozen stupor for judgement day.

And I still wait,
And another winter knocks,
I ready myself
For endless nights,
Cruel in their deception,
Killing innocents in their wake.
I dream of the summer sun,
Summer of eternal freedom--
The smiles of children,
Music and harmony,
An equal sound
Of joy and brotherhood--
A chorus of togetherness.

When I awake one day soon,
To the welcome breeze
Of open doors,

I know I will see them free,
Of ignorance and bigotry
Far from the clutches
Of this travesty.

15. Memory is an Egyptian tomb

Basking in lightness,
Lolling in the haze--
Comfortably numbed,
Eyes fixed
On a maze.
Little holes in a grill
In the ceiling--
White seems to be
The order of the day.
Like washed out pictures,
Do memories fade away?

I am a mummy
Embalmed and static,
The perforations provide
An ethereal escape
From the mundane.
Or is it otherwise?
Twists and turns--

This my life,
Sometimes serpentine,
Has been quite the ride!

Mummified memories
Parade for my pleasure--
People, places, things.
I am a delirious dummy
With a total recall
of experience!
Was it all just for this?
A long beep and a blip
Zilch, Naught, Nada?

But memories are like
A Pharaoh's tomb,
Glistening in the moonlight,
Whispering to the night.
Across empty halls
They call out
Like statues came to life,
Coming around in single file--
They perform one last time
For my benefit.

And like a Pharaoh,
I will leave

My sleeping shell,
My scattered artefacts,
And proceed
To the next dimension.
I will exit
My cozy sarcophagus,
And ascend
The steps of my Pyramid,
Toward the open sky,
To enter the amazing Afterlife!

16. A Gambler's life

A game of cards,
A pack of lies,
The die is cast
Amidst silent sighs.

The poker faces,
The shaded eyes,
The bated breath,
Then the surprise!

The smoke is thick,
Their silence is gold,
Yet the busy den
Is a sight to behold.

The men are dusty
From their work all day,
This is their time

To pay and play!

Their faces are etched
With lines of time,
They drink and hope
In this pantomime.

Is this the night when
Fortune smiles,
And will someone
Walk away with the prize?

Or will hell break loose
With the bullet's sound?
Silence shattered,
Body on the ground?

Will a winning man
Lose to fate?
And will sport end
In greed and hate?

The saloons tell
Many a tale
Of gamblers from hell,
Over smokes and ale.

The Russian Roulette
Plagues all and one.
Life ends like a gamble,
Whether it's lost or won!

17. What I am

At heart I am a sailor,
Sailing in my boat.
Waiting to touch
The next sunny port.
Anticipating the pleasure
Of setting my eyes
On foreign shores.

At heart I am a wanderer,
Even as I sit
In my cozy chair, I yearn
For unknown climes and countries
And landscapes
I have not seen.

At heart I am a teacher,
I wish to leave a roadmap
Of where to venture,
And where not to tread
On the path that is
Familiar to me.

At heart I am a student,
Ever eager and curious.
Disciplined and laborious,
Happy with the fruits
Of my devotion

I could have been a preacher,
But I'm too earthly-bound
I could have been a joker
Or an actor with a mask
But am I too earnest
And handicapped somewhat,
With this wound that I hide?
I could have been an activist,
But I quietly nurse my wound.

I would if I could.
But I did not
Become any of these.

18. Message for Mother

You did not say goodbye,
Or did you?
Was that a tear
In your eye,
A shadow of fear, maybe.

You made your way,
Without a word,
Without turning back,
Or pausing a moment
To say
You were leaving me.

You disappeared,
Just went away.
I turned the corner,
You were not there.
I looked back,
And saw nothingness.

Now with a tremble in my legs,
And an empty heart,
I take baby steps once more
Into this world, Mother,
And you are not here with me.

19. Innocence

A baby's eyes,
A trust that I cannot betray--
An innocence that reminds me
Of a forgotten day so long ago
When we played and ran,
Danced and pretended,
In gardens green with song,
With no cares or places to go
In a hurried sort of way.

Though I love that watery gaze,
Like pure light glints in a crystal ball,
It makes me want to look away,
For I am reminded of a day
When our only work was play.
Unknown were the ways of men,
And labour, a nasty stranger.

We only knew our playful den
And cats and dogs and children.
And our garden of delights
Was made of creatures,
Toys, and childish fights.

Infancy and childhood,
Are like a glass cocoon,
Lit by the silver moon,
Warmed by the golden sun
Of innocence--
Peering into a forgotten world,
In the dark and lonely night,
We can only look from far
With our scratchy, worn out lens.

20. Solitude

Solitude
Is like a familiar friend
I welcome in
With open arms.
He always comes
With food and cheer
And lots of rest.
He chats with me
In foreign tongues.
We read and ponder,
Watch a film.
I miss society less and less,
As we grow close.
Like an invisible jester
He entertains--
There's always something
In his bag of tricks.
As I grow older I like him more--

He has no pretence,
No tantrums, and I
Could be petulant or sad,
Excited or a bore,
He wouldn't leave my side.
I like his motley company.
Imagine being stuck
With an unwanted friend!

We travel together
In time and space,
And we dance
In our imaginary square,
We fall in line,
We match our steps,
Skipping and gambolling
We catch our crowd--
Reliving dreams and memories
In our carnival of shadows.

21. Serpentine

Like a serpent
Uncoiling
From a muddled heap
You rise,
Lighting my wheels
In a lightning strike!
A cracker spinning
On a festive night!
Red, orange, yellow,
Indigo, blue and green,
Race in a line
Along my spine,
And silently explode
In a bloom
In my crown--
The violet jewel
That encapsulates
My being and becoming.
Enveloped in a silent chaos
Of white light,

Still, and vibrating in ecstasy,
Kundalini,
Your serpentine embrace
Sends me soaring
To the flashpoint,
Connecting to the instant.
Beyond the darting tongues
Of your icy fire,
My eye, half-open, sees
The zero of eternity!

www.ingramcontent.com/pod-product-compliance
Lightning Source LLC
Chambersburg PA
CBHW070457050426
42449CB00012B/3016